GARDEN GUIDES

CLEMATIS &
CLIMBERS

GARDEN GUIDES

CLEMATIS &
CLIMBERS

LANCE HATTATT

Illustrations by
ELAINE FRANKS

CHARTWELL
BOOKS, INC.

Published by Chartwell Books
a division of Book Sales, Inc.
114 Northfield Avenue
Edison, NJ 08837

This edition produced for sale
in the U.S.A., its territories
and dependencies only.

ISBN 0-7858-0535-4

Produced by Robert Ditchfield Ltd

Printed and bound in Italy

CONTENTS

POISONOUS PLANTS

In recent years, concern has been voiced about poisonous plants or plants which can cause allergic reactions if touched. The fact is that many plants are poisonous, some in a particular part, others in all their parts. For the sake of safety, it is always, without exception, essential to assume that no part of a plant should be eaten unless it is known, without any doubt whatsoever, that the plant or its part is edible and that it cannot provoke an allergic reaction in the individual person who samples it. It must also be remembered that some plants can cause severe dermatitis, blistering or an allergic reaction if touched, in some individuals and not in others. It is the responsibility of the individual to take all the above into account.

How to Use This Book

Where appropriate, approximate measurements of a plant's height have been given, and also the spread where this is significant, in both metric and imperial measures. The height is the first measurement, as for example 1.2m × 60cm/4 × 2ft. However, both height and spread vary so greatly from garden to garden since they depend on soil, climate and position, that these measurements are offered as guides only. This is especially true of trees and shrubs where ultimate growth can be unpredictable.

The following symbols are also used throughout the book:

    ◯ = thrives best or only in full sun
    ◑ = thrives best or only in part-shade
    ● = succeeds in full shade
    E = evergreen

Where no sun symbol and no reference to sun or shade is made in the text, it can be assumed that the plant tolerates sun or light shade.

Plant Names

For ease of reference this book gives the botanical name under which a plant is most widely listed for the gardener. These names are sometimes changed and in such cases the new name has been included. Common names are given wherever they are in frequent use.

CLEMATIS AND CLIMBERS

CLEMATIS AND CLIMBERS are the soft furnishings of the garden. They contribute a luxuriant, well-appointed effect, adding both height and interest. Additionally, where used to climb through trees and shrubs they extend the season of the host plant. The introduction of climbers into a small garden, where space is restricted and therefore at a premium, greatly increases the range of plants to be grown.

WHICH CLIMBER?

Whatever the situation, however difficult, a climber is available to meet all but the most impossible of requirements. Evergreen ivies, many with bright, variegated foliage, will often flourish in dry, shady conditions where the soil is poor and thin. The shelter of a wall, perhaps that of the house, will allow many less hardy subjects to be grown with considerable success. Against a much frequented path the fragrance of a scented honeysuckle may be enjoyed to the full. For interest over an extended period the small-flowered clematis which later carry fluffy seedheads are an excellent choice. A conservatory or glasshouse where a constant temperature is maintained

Above: *Clematis* 'Fireworks' grows over a tall wooden quadripod.
Opposite: *Clematis* 'Perle d'Azur' makes a wonderful display in late summer as a backcloth to a seat.

during colder months will allow all manner of tender climbers to be grown.

POSITIONING FOR EFFECT

A walk around the garden should suggest numerous places to position climbers. House and garage walls, boundary hedges and fences, the sides of sheds and summerhouses, railings, even unsightly washing-line posts

Clematis and honeysuckle intertwine to great effect, but the honeysuckle must be watched in case it throttles its partner.

will all become apparent. Other supports may need to be constructed: arbour, arch, column, pergola, pyramid or trellis. Some natural features will be enhanced with the addition of a climber. A rose spilling out of an ancient apple tree is a delight in midsummer. Partner the rose with a clematis and the effect is even more stunning. Teaming large-flowered clematis with the foliage of shrubs provides countless permutations and enviable results.

Climbers do not, of course, have to be grown vertically. Many may be trained horizontally through the borders, by pegging to the earth, to create unusual and original schemes.

SUITABLE SITES

Correct growing conditions will ensure healthy, successful plants. Before planting it is advisable to introduce and work in generous quantities of well rotted manure or garden

10

Clematis 'Hagley Hybrid' and *Hydrangea anomala petiolaris*.

Rosa 'Madame Grégoire Staechelin' and *Wisteria floribunda*.

compost. During dry periods plants should be kept well watered until they are fully established. When positioning a climber against a wall, ascertain that any roof overhang does not preclude rain reaching the roots. Clematis, particularly, are rich feeders and will welcome an annual top dressing of organic matter.

Some climbers are self-supporting, ivies for example; others will require tying-in. A cane positioned at the base of the plant and directed towards the host will encourage shoots in the desired direction. Such supports should be put in place at the time of planting to avoid damage to the plant's root system. All ties should be checked regularly and not allowed to cut into stems. Smooth surfaces can be faced with plastic-coated mesh, chicken wire or studded with fastenings to assist young tendrils.

11

Tropaeolum speciosum (Flame flower) glows against a yew hedge.

CARING FOR CLIMBERS

Once established many climbers will require little attention beyond checking ties, eliminating dead wood, the thinning of over-crowded branches and an annual feed. Indeed, pruning should not be regarded as a potential problem but rather as a matter of common sense. More often than not it is sufficient simply to maintain a healthy framework, taking out spindly or diseased stems. As a general rule of thumb, little harm will result from pruning immediately after flowering.

Clematis are often regarded as a special case. Contrary to popular belief, pruning techniques are not at all complicated. Early-flowering clematis require little pruning beyond the removal of weak and dead stems once flowering is over. Large-flowered hybrids, blooming before midsummer, should be lightly pruned, which involves removing tangled growth and generally thinning-out after flowering. Those flowering later, on the current season's stems, should be cut back hard to ground level during the winter months. New, young shoots will shortly appear.

COMPANION PLANTINGS

Climbers should be used in profusion, with generosity of spirit. Team them with trees, with shrubs and with each other. Use as ground cover or as a focal point in pots and containers. Have them cascading down and scaling heights. Planted in these ways the most wonderful and original effects can be realized. Planting schemes are limitless; with a little experimentation the most exciting

Many climbers are unfussy about situation. Others will require certain conditions to be satisfied. It may be the protection of a warm wall, safeguarding new shoots against slugs or, as in the case of clematis, shading roots from the sun. For this a large stone placed at the base of the plant should be adequate. Planting instructions should be heeded.

12

Rosa 'Zéphirine Drouhin' is planted to make a screen, a charming feature that is of medieval origin.

combinations can be achieved.

There can be no hard and fast rules. White flowers look startlingly brilliant against the dark green of a clipped yew hedge. Red flowers, such as those of the scarlet *Tropaeolum speciosum*, in the same situation make a very different, but equally powerful, kind of statement. Pale pinks in semi-shade gleam with a luminosity, dark pinks in full sun demand to be noticed. Purple on gold is distinctive, purple mixed with grey is moody and Gothic. Imagination and a sense of purpose are the only requirements to transform the garden into something exceptional, extraordinary and very beautiful.

1. CLEMATIS

Add a touch of sophistication to any garden scene with the inclusion of a lovely flowered clematis.

TINY NODDING HEADS of the delightful alpina and macropetala clematis are amongst the first to appear. Grown through shrubs, which will flower later in the year, or to scramble into evergreen trees, they add an extra and welcome dimension.

This Ali Baba jar would make an excellent subject for a patio or any sitting-out area. Here the pretty pink heads of *Clematis alpina* **'Ruby'** and the blue *C. alpina* **'Frances Rivis'** jostle over the edges.

Clematis alpina will grow very happily in a cool, shady situation and be amongst the first to flower.

Clematis alpina 'Frances Rivis' A slightly larger cultivar of semi-double, mid-blue flowers.

◆ *Both* Clematis alpina *and* macropetala *types are suitable for growing as ground cover.*

Clematis macropetala 'Maidwell Hall' Violet blue flowers contrast with the lime green bracts of *Euphorbia amygdaloides robbiae*.

Clematis cirrhosa An evergreen producing welcome blooms in late winter.

Clematis macropetala 'Blue Bird' Fresh foliage complements the clear blue of this early spring flower.

AN EARLY SHOW

Clematis armandii Evergreen clematis, very vigorous, early and long-flowering (see also PLANTS WITH PERFUME)

CLIMBING HEIGHTS

No ultimate heights are given for clematis. These will depend on area, aspect, situation and soil type. Nearly all can be controlled and contained with regular pruning.

Most clematis will tolerate sun or shade, though their roots must always be shaded. Some flowers, like those of the popular large-flowered 'Nelly Moser', fade less if they are out of the sun.

AN EARLY SHOW

PRUNING THE MONTANAS

Flowering during the early spring, *Clematis montana* and its various forms need little in the way of pruning. Young plants may be cut back to around 1m/3ft immediately after they have flowered. Established plants should have dead or weak stems removed after the flowering period. Flowers form on new shoots, so if you prune later you will remove the following year's display.

***Clematis* 'Wada's Primrose'** A deliciously pale and creamy hybrid requiring no more than a light prune.

Clematis montana This most attractive clematis remains understandably popular. It looks especially good in the evening light.

***Clematis montana* 'Elizabeth'** A charming, free-flowering form, the flowers of which are vanilla scented.

***Clematis montana* 'Rubens'** Mauve-pink flowers reflect the purple hues of the new growth of the young leaves.

Clematis chrysocoma makes a very acceptable alternative to the more vigorous montanas where space is restricted. A profusion of soft pink flowers are displayed against downy foliage which is slightly bronze tinted.

◆ *Little pruning is required. After flowering cut back to desired width and height.*

REACHING UP INTO A TREE or tumbling over a wall, *Clematis montana* and its various forms are an excellent choice. Growing to several metres, in full flower they form a white or pink cascade of hundreds of starry blooms.

Clematis montana **'Tetrarose'** The deep pink of this form shows up brilliantly against the royal blue of *Ceanothus* 'Puget Blue'.

◆ *Be careful about growing montana clematis over shrubs; they can easily smother and kill them.*

BOLD *and* BEAUTIFUL

Clematis 'Guernsey Cream'
The depth and richness of
this cream clematis is most
marked against a dark
background. Early summer.

Clematis 'Miss Crawshay'
Mauve-pink flowers are
rather silky in appearance.
Early summer.

◆ *This clematis is ideal for
a restricted space as it
seldom exceeds 2m/6ft.*

**Clematis 'Étoile de
Malicorne'** A distinctive
and unusual clematis which
here is being trained
horizontally. Early summer.

Clematis 'Lincoln Star' A
wonderful true pink
clematis with flowers as
much as 15cm/6in across.
Early summer.

Clematis 'Ville de Lyon'
This clematis is a popular
choice as it is scarcely
without flower during the
summer months.

◆ *For early blooms, prune
lightly. To restrict growth to
around 3m/10ft, hard
prune.*

Clematis 'Elsa Späth' Not a
difficult plant to grow and
one which flowers very
freely. Early summer.

MOST SPECTACULAR OF ALL CLEMATIS are the large-flowered hybrids. For drama and impact these must be the first choice. Single, double or semi-double, they are available in a range of shapes, sizes and colours to suit all situations and tastes. Main flowering season is given though the blooms are often recurrent.

***Clematis* 'Lady Northcliffe'** The attraction of this deep lavender blue clematis must be linked with its vigour. Midsummer.

***Clematis* 'Kathleen Wheeler'** Large plummy-mauve flowers pleasantly fade as the blooms go over. Midsummer.

Here the deep wine red of ***Clematis* 'Madame Edouard André'** associates with the clear blue of the ever popular ***Clematis* 'Perle d'Azur'**. Both should be pruned hard in the early part of the year.

Bold *and* Beautiful

Clematis **'Barbara Dibley'** A moderate grower with flowers of deep red fading, as here, to pale magenta. Early summer.

Clematis **'Barbara Jackman'** Superb colour, elegant shape and vigorous, healthy growth in this marvellous plant. Early summer.

Clematis **'Fireworks'** As its name suggests, 'Fireworks' is indeed most exciting and dramatic. Early summer.

Clematis **'Mrs George Jackman'** Not dissimilar in appearance to 'Marie Boisselot' but rather creamier. Early summer.

Clematis **'Vino'** This full-bodied clematis is aptly named. Seldom seen, it is worth looking out for. Early summer.

Clematis **'Marie Boisselot'** Absolutely lovely for its sheer whiteness once the large flowers have fully opened. Midsummer.

◆ *'Marie Boisselot' is sometimes sold as 'Madame le Coultre'. The two plants are identical.*

***Clematis* 'Duchess of Sutherland'** Carmine-red blooms are produced on the current season's growth. Midsummer.

***Clematis* 'Miss Bateman'** The purple leaves of the cotinus are a perfect foil to the attractive flower heads. Early summer.

***Clematis* 'Jackmanii Superba'** Superior to *Clematis jackmanii* in that the flowers are larger and the sepals broader. Late summer.

***Clematis* 'Victoria'** seen here in contrast to the pronounced yellow of *Hemerocallis* 'Whichford'. Late summer.

***Clematis* 'Comtesse de Bouchaud'** Pearly mauve-pink flowers which shine through the foliage of host trees or shrubs. Late summer.

◆ *This vigorous clematis is deservedly popular with its masses of blooms.*

***Clematis* 'Niobe'** Ruby red flowers to adorn a wall or host shrub. Early summer.

BOLD *and* BEAUTIFUL

CONTAINER-GROWN CLEMATIS provide infinite variety and possibility. Use them to enliven a dreary corner, to make a show on a terrace or patio or simply as an opportunity to cultivate where no open ground is available.

POT-GROWN CLEMATIS

All clematis enjoy rich growing conditions.

Ensure good drainage by filling the bottom of the pot with a generous layer of crocks. If possible raise the container off the ground to prevent blockage.

Keep well watered at all times, particularly during dry periods.

Clematis **'Mrs Cholmondeley'** Hard pruning will result in flowers from midsummer onwards, otherwise early flowering.

Clematis **'Mrs P.B. Truax'** Wonderfully silky flowers demand to be touched. The main flowering period is early summer.

Clematis **'Nelly Moser'** One of the best known and loved of all clematis and a prolific flowerer. Early summer.

◆ *To avoid unnecessary fading, keep out of full sun.*

Clematis 'Hagley Hybrid'
Rarely without a plentiful
supply of pale mauve-pink
flowers which come on new
growth. Late summer.

◆ *As a popular alternative,
grow* **_'Lady Northcliffe'_** *in a
container.*

Clematis 'The President'
Still widely grown after a
period of more than 100
years. Early summer.

◆ *'Vyvyan Pennell' shares
the same colour tones but is
double flowered.*

Clematis 'Arctic Queen' is seen here fully
clothing a wooden pyramid with a mass of
unusual double flowers. Early summer.

◆ *A simple wooden pyramid is the best
way to train clematis in a pot.*

BOLD *and* BEAUTIFUL

Always shade the roots of clematis with a stone slab, thick mulch or another plant. Plant 10cm/4in deeper than in the container as insurance against wilt.

FLOWER BOWERS ARE CREATED when large-flowered clematis are allowed to festoon arbours and arches. A pergola draped in clematis and roses produces a magical garden feature. For a simple effect, smother a free-standing pot.

Clematis '**Duchess of Edinburgh**' A wonderful double, pure white but sadly not always easy to establish. Early summer.

Clematis '**Mme Edouard André**' Slow growth habit makes this clematis suitable for a small space or pot. Late summer.

Clematis '**W.E. Gladstone**' Exceedingly large flowers of up to 25cm/10in. Midsummer.

Clematis '**Ernest Markham**' is amongst the strongest growers of the large-flowered hybrids. Late summer.

◆ *Position in full sun to encourage the greatest number of flowers.*

Clematis 'Maureen' A comparatively modern clematis introduced during the 1950s. For best results, prune lightly. Midsummer.

Clematis 'Lord Nevill' One of the most intensely blue of all clematis with a second flowering in autumn. Early summer.

Clematis 'Perle d'Azur' It is not difficult to understand the widespread appeal of this beautiful clematis. Late summer.

Clematis 'Rouge Cardinal' Deep crimson flowers of a velvet texture which disappointingly fade. Late summer.

Clematis 'Pink Champagne' Well named, for the flower seems to possess an extravagant, fun-loving quality. Early summer.

Clematis 'Gipsy Queen' Deep purple flowers are seen here growing with **Clematis viticella 'Purpurea Plena Elegans'**. Late summer.

◆ *This picture shows the top of an arch which bears a mass of bloom over a long period.*

Clematis *rehderiana* An absolute delight when the delicate, fragrant flowers are arranged to fall at eye level. Late.

◆ *Cut hard back to the ground in the spring. Resulting growth will reach 2.4–3m/8–10ft.*

Clematis *recta* is an herbaceous perennial growing up to 2m/6ft in a season. It may require some support. Midsummer.

Clematis *florida* 'Alba Plena' Surely one of the most desirable of all clematis for its lovely greenish-white blooms. Late.

◆ *Afford this clematis the protection of a warm wall or grow as a conservatory plant.*

SOME CLEMATIS ARE ESPECIALLY DISTINGUISHED. They are the aristocrats, seldom seen, stylish, rather covetable and deserve a choice position in the garden where their worth may be readily appreciated.

Clematis × *aromatica* The lemony scent of this rather charming little flower is somewhat evasive but worth pursuing.

Clematis × *eriostemon* **'Hendersonii'** An excellent subject to encourage as light ground cover through the border. Late.

Clematis **'Burma Star'** For an effective contrast, train this clematis through a gold-leafed shrub. Midsummer.

BUYING WISELY

The more unusual clematis will, very naturally, be rather more expensive. It is important, therefore, that care is taken over selection.

Do not necessarily choose the tallest in the pot. Instead look for strong growth and a healthy appearance.

In winter check for prominent swelling leaf axil buds towards the base of the stem.

Clematis florida **'Sieboldii'** Often mistaken for a passion flower, the joy of this appealing clematis is the deep purple centre set against creamy sepals. Position in a sunny spot or, alternatively, grow as a container specimen. Late.

CHOICE CLEMATIS

LATE-FLOWERING TEXENSIS HYBRIDS are delightful climbers to incorporate into the garden scene. Rather like miniature, hanging tulips they make a lovely addition to specimen shrubs. Prune in early spring. Remove all the previous year's growth and cut above a new leaf bud close to the ground.

***Clematis texensis* 'Etoile Rose'** Possibly the loveliest of all the texensis varieties, though seldom seen.

◆ *Texensis clematis require hard pruning early in the year.*

***Clematis texensis* 'Duchess of Albany'** Rose pink bars provide additional interest to the extended bell-shaped flowers.

***Clematis texensis* 'The Princess of Wales'** Deep pink trumpet flowers make a fine addition to many planting schemes.

***Clematis texensis* 'Gravetye Beauty'** From midsummer onwards rich red flowers unfold into star shapes.

***Clematis texensis* 'Sir Trevor Lawrence'** Brilliant crimson flowers with violet shading.

TO GIVE THE GARDEN SOMETHING SPECIAL, seek out those clematis which are less often cultivated. Most are easy to grow and will reward with exciting, unusual blooms.

Clematis '**Lady Londesborough**' As the flowers tend to come together, this is a plant for a showy situation. Early.

Clematis '**Arabella**' Allow this charming little clematis to scramble at will amongst pastel summer flowers.

Clematis × *durandii* Somewhat reluctant to climb, *durandii* is at its best given the support of a twiggy shrub. Midsummer.

Clematis forsteri Afford some shelter to this wonderfully fragrant, early flowering, evergreen clematis.

Clematis '**Henryi**' One of the oldest large-flowered hybrids to remain in cultivation. Midsummer.

Clematis '**Royalty**' Rich purple tones befit this aptly named hybrid. Early.

Clematis '**Dr. Ruppel**' A good, strong grower which flowers freely throughout the summer.

◆ *Bold hues of this kind need careful placement.*

A delightful combination is achieved in this garden scene by placing together the two late flowerers *Clematis* **'Huldine'** and *Clematis viticella* **'Royal Velours'**. Here the stone balustrade provides a ready-made support.

LATE PERFORMERS

Clematis tangutica This yellow flowered species is well known, well liked and widely grown.

As THE YEAR PROGRESSES and the blooms of many of the large-flowered hybrids go over, so they are replaced with those clematis which will provide a point of interest for late summer into autumn. Most noticeable are the orientalis, tangutica and viticella types.

Clematis viticella 'Elvan' An absolutely stunning display in which the warm purple flowers complement the grey stone. In this case the addition of a wire frame gives extra support.

Clematis 'Viticella Rubra' Formerly named 'Kermesina' this variety has bright crimson flowers.

Clematis viticella 'Madame Julia Correvon' A beautiful deep red shade to bring colour towards the close of season.

Clematis 'Lasurstern' Although less prolific than earlier in the season, 'Lasurstern' will flower reliably at the year's end.

LATE PERFORMERS

FLUFFY SEEDHEADS ARE AN END-OF-SEASON BONUS. Some, like those of *tangutica*, will survive the winter whilst others are fascinating in themselves. At this time the foliage of the early flowering montanas incorporates purple tints.

***Clematis viticella* 'Purpurea Plena Elegans'** A double flower which, because of its smallness, is especially appealing.

◆ *These flowers are an ideal match for the plum coloured fruits of* Callicarpa bodinieri giraldii.

***Clematis × jouiniana* 'Praecox'** A non-clinging clematis which should be allowed to roam at will.

***Clematis heracleifolia* 'Davidiana'** The flowers of this herbaceous clematis are heavily scented and are borne to the year's end.

***Clematis heracleifolia* 'Wyevale'** Cut herbaceous clematis back to the ground at the season's close.

***Clematis viticella* 'Etoile Violette'** will, when established, flower to the point of almost obscuring the foliage.

Clematis viticella '**Margot Koster**' Very floriferous with brilliant, narrow magenta sepals.

CLEMATIS WILT

The main symptom of wilt is the sudden collapse of an otherwise healthy plant. Treatment should include the removal to the ground of all diseased material, the application of a sulphur-based fungicide, a mulch of fresh compost and copious watering.

Always plant the root-ball of clematis up to 10cm/4in deeper than the soil-level in the container to enable it to throw up new shoots from below the level of the soil, if it has been affected by the disease.

These lingering seedheads have a quiet charm long after the flowers are forgotten.

Clematis campaniflora Hard pruning will result in a profusion of understated but elegant flowers.

Clematis viticella '**Mary Rose**' A highly desirable clematis, well worth seeking out.

Clematis viticella '**Alba Luxurians**' Placing this delightful variety would pose few problems.

2. CLIMBING ROSES

Scrambling over arches, clothing mellow brick or reaching up into ancient trees, the climbing roses possess a timeless beauty.

PASTEL SHADES

QUIET PINKS, pale lemons, mauves, peaches and apricots, these muted colours create a mood of tranquillity. Use them individually to add height to a soft-hued scheme or teamed to dress up a walkway.

Rosa 'Paul's Lemon Pillar' Strong growth, huge lemony white flowers and fine perfume. 6m/20ft

Rosa 'Paul's Himalayan Musk' Dainty sprays of blush blooms in midsummer. 9m/30ft

◆ *This is a strong grower and can cover a tree.*

Rosa 'Albertine' Deservedly popular, this splendid near double rose is heavily fragrant. 5.5m/18ft

◆ *Train 'Albertine' against a wall or permit it to scramble among shrubs.*

Rosa **'Madame Grégoire Staechelin'** Plant this against a sunless wall and experience thèse wonderful, early, fleshy blooms. 6m/20ft

Rosa **'Souvenir de la Malmaison Climber'** This beautiful blush rose flowers twice, the second crop being the better. 3.5m/12ft

Rosa **'Veilchenblau'** Violet petals streaked white, later fading to lilac-grey. Suitable for shade. 3.5m/12ft

◆ *In this formal situation 'Veilchenblau' is trained as an arch above yew hedges.*

PASTEL SHADES

Rosa 'May Queen'
Completely unfussy with regard to position, in flower 'May Queen' is a mass of bloom. 4.5m/15ft

THE ROSE is often thought of as the Queen of Climbers. Perhaps more than anything else it has become the symbol of summer, the garden at its peak. Climbing roses are not demanding plants to grow. Give them a fertilizer when planting, repeat as necessary and mulch in spring to conserve moisture.

Rosa 'Débutante' Dating back to 1902, this lovely clear rose pink flower cannot fail but to please. 4.5m/15ft

◆ *Not only is this rose delightfully fragrant but it is also excellent as a cut flower.*

Rosa 'Lady Waterlow' The clear pink flowers are salmon shaded and pleasantly scented. 3.5m/12ft

◆ *This climbing Hybrid Tea rose flowers early summer and often again in late summer.*

Rosa 'Blairii Number Two' makes a spectacular show when grown as a feature in the border. 4.5m/15ft

◆ *Most Old roses are grown for their display in midsummer.*

Rosa anemonoides The simplicity of this single, soft pink rose is totally appealing. It requires a sheltered spot. 2.4m/8ft

PRUNING

Any pruning to be carried out is best left until late winter. At that time the removal or shortening of wood that has flowered will encourage new growth for the coming season. Occasionally old wood may be removed from the base to let in light and air. New shoots at the base should be allowed to develop as replacements.

Rosa 'Albéric Barbier' Soft yellow flowers later become creamy white. It is rarely without some flower. 6m/20ft

◆ *'Albéric Barbier' will tolerate more shade than most roses.*

HOT *and* SMOKY

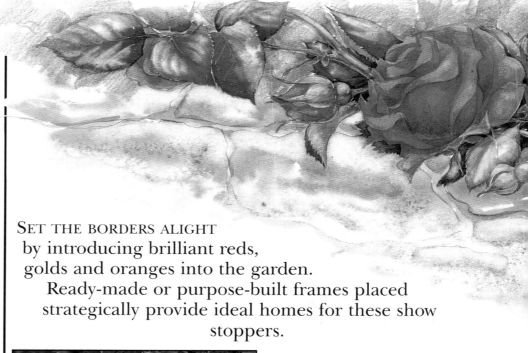

SET THE BORDERS ALIGHT
by introducing brilliant reds,
golds and oranges into the garden.
Ready-made or purpose-built frames placed
strategically provide ideal homes for these show
stoppers.

Rosa **'Golden Showers'** is an excellent choice to grow up and around a pillar or self-standing support. 2.4m/8ft

Rosa **'Maigold'** Less inclined to climb, 'Maigold' is seen at its best when used to clothe low shrubs. 3.5m/12ft

Rosa **'Bleu Magenta'** Darkest of dark, violet-crimson, double flowers convey a sense of deepening mystery. 4.5m/15ft.

Rosa **'Paul's Scarlet Climber'** This most striking crimson-scarlet rose is, not surprisingly, widely grown. 3.5m/12ft

A blaze of colour is
achieved when the
double orange-scarlet blooms
of *Rosa* **'Danse du Feu'**
intermingle with the deep yellow
of *Clematis tangutica*. The bronze
tinted foliage of this spirited
modern climbing rose adds lustre.

ICE COOL

CREAM AND WHITE ROSES suggest flowery bowers. As a centrepiece to an all-white garden, to climb into old fruit trees or to garland ropes, the choice is immense.

Rosa 'Sanders' White' deserves a place in every garden where its true beauty can readily be appreciated. 2.4m/8ft

◆ Viola cornuta *happily extends the white theme in this garden.*

Rosa 'Iceberg' The climbing form of this floribunda carries masses of pure white flowers over shining leaves. 3m/10ft

Rosa 'Rambling Rector' This is a rose to grow through old trees where vigour can be left unchecked. 10m/33ft

Rosa 'Félicité et Perpétue' is a classic rose whose double rosette flowers are a constant source of pleasure. 3.5m/12ft

Care should be taken when considering **Rosa filipes 'Kiftsgate'**. This extraordinary rose has enormous growth potential and is only suitable where space really is unlimited.

◆ *Seen here as a wonderful white cascade through foxgloves, 'Kiftsgate' has individual shoots of 6m/20ft or more.*

3. CLIMBERS FOR FOLIAGE AND FLOWER

*Combine the form and texture of leaves
with understated flowers for dramatic
and impressive effects.*

Wisterias remain one of the most popular and, indeed, one of the most charming of all climbers. In addition to attractive, fresh green foliage and beautiful flower racemes, mature plants are noted for their interesting, gnarled wood.

***Wisteria floribunda* 'Alba'** Cascades of pure white flowers pour down this house wall in early summer. ○, 9m/30ft

◆ *Try growing* Wisteria floribunda *above bearded irises to flower at the same time.*

***Wisteria sinensis* 'Caroline'** Impossible to resist. Sinensis forms are amongst the most fragrant of all. ○, 30m/100ft

VARIEGATED LEAVES, patterned foliage, simple, unassuming flowers and even twisted branches are but a few of the reasons why some climbers are valued throughout the year. These are not necessarily plants for centre stage but ones which perform an important, supporting rôle.

Most climbers, except the most vigorous, can be contained by regular pruning to fit within a given space but it is unwise to plant those that grow far and fast in a confined position.

Jasminum nudiflorum remains attractive even when leafless in winter. Winter jasmine is ideal for training. 2.4m/8ft

Chaenomeles × superba 'Rowallane' These pretty flowers will continue well after the leaves are fully out. 1m/3ft

Chaenomeles speciosa 'Nivalis' (Japonica, flowering quince) White flowers on bare stems will later be followed by traditional quinces. 2m/6ft

Actinidia kolomikta has unusual leaves which, grown in full sun, are splashed pink and white. 3.5m/12ft

ALL-YEAR INTEREST

Hedera helix **'Cristata'**
Exceedingly prettily shaped leaves are the mark of this distinguished ivy. E, 2.7m/9ft

Hedera helix **'Buttercup'** A magnificent yellow-leafed form which must be grown in sun to maintain colour. E, 2.7m/9ft

IVIES ARE AMONGST THE MOST VERSATILE of climbers, self-clinging and growing in almost every situation including deep shade. Not all are as hungry for space as the common ivy, *Hedera helix*, nor as plain. Very often the shape of the leaves and the degree of variegation make these the most diverse of evergreens.

In this garden, ivy is used with ceanothus to make a substantial and pleasing screen.

◆ *Growth is easily restricted with a severe pruning in spring.*

Hedera helix **'Goldheart'** is a small-leafed ivy with enormous vigour but apt to revert to green. E, 2.7m/9ft

Hedera colchica **'Sulphur Heart'** Brilliant variegation on large leaves lightens up the gloomiest corner. E, 4.5m/15ft

SOMETIMES IT BECOMES NECESSARY TO MASK or hide an unsightly building such as a garden shed or a garage. As well as ivy, a number of other climbers are readily suited to this task.

Polygonum baldschuanicum
The Russian vine, or mile-a-minute, will smother any structure in a short while. ○, 12m/39ft

Hydrangea anomala petiolaris This climbing hydrangea will thrive on a sunless wall. Self-clinging. 8m/26ft

Lathyrus grandiflorus The everlasting pea carries numerous magenta pea-flowers. ○, 1.5m/5ft

Lonicera sempervirens A leafy honeysuckle with brilliant flowers all summer long. ◑, E or semi E, 4m/13ft

Hollies are especially appealing at this time of the year, their glossy berries warming up drab days. Many are eminently suitable for clipping to form spiky screens or barriers. Here *Ilex aquifolium* '**J C van Tol**' has almost spineless leaves with abundant red berries.

BRIGHT BERRIES AND BURNISHED LEAVES conjure up the sights, sounds and smells of autumn. Virginia creepers lit by a dying sun, purple-leafed vines and spent golden hops are all late players.

Pyracantha in its many forms will produce a mass of bright berries in autumn. E, 2.1m/7ft

◆ *Around this cottage the trained pyracantha has formed part of the architecture.*

Parthenocissus henryana Dark crimson leaves (bronze-green in spring and summer) capture the essence of autumn in this self-clinging creeper. ◑, ●, 10m/33ft

Vitis coignetiae The crimson glory vine is trained in this instance around a pillar. Leaves are gradually turning from green to deep wine red. 15m/49ft

Parthenocissus tricuspidata **'Veitchii'** The Boston ivy will in time cover a large area, supporting itself with self-clinging tendrils. 20m/66ft

53

CLIMBERS *with* STYLE

Asarina antirrhiniflora
Grown as an annual, this pretty climbing snapdragon is not often seen in gardens. ○, 1.5m/5ft

Convolvulus althaeoides
Well suited to scramble over low walls. Pretty but tender and needs frost protection. ○, 1m/3ft

Lonicera × tellmanniana
Although lacking scent this honeysuckle has really bold orange-yellow flowers.
◑ 5m/16ft

***Lathyrus latifolius* 'White Pearl'** An excellent white form of the everlasting pea to include in almost any planting. ○, 2m/6ft

***Cobaea scandens/ C. s.* 'Alba'** An elegant pairing of two fast-growing half-hardy climbers. ○, 4–5m/13–16ft.

◆ *Bushy growth is encouraged by pinching out growing tips.*

Wattakaka sinensis This is a climber to add interest to an arch or pergola. Plant in sun. E, 2.7m/9ft

***Ipomoea* 'Early Call'** (Morning glory) A splendid and exotic-looking half-hardy climber to flower for the entire summer. ○, 3m/10ft

SOME GARDEN SITUATIONS demand special treatment. It may be that a dominant mood or theme requires extending. These climbers, used with imagination and thought, will do just that.

Dicentra torulosa An unusual, annual dicentra with clusters of flowers followed by interesting seed pods. 3m/10ft

Aconitum volubile A climbing monkshood. Lilac-purple flowers are produced from late summer. 3m/10ft

Tropaeolum speciosum makes a magnificent show of scarlet when grown against a dark background. 2m/6ft

◆ *Occasionally the flowers are followed by deep blue berries from which new plants can be grown.*

CLIMBERS *with* STYLE

SUN AND THE SHELTER OF A PROTECTING WALL are necessary for some of these elegant, classic climbers. In such a spot they will perform well with wonderful, impressive foliage and flowers.

Ribes speciosum The fuchsia-flowered currant is at its best against a light background as shown here. ○, 2.4m/8ft

◆ *Dark shiny foliage, rich red, sophisticated fuchsia-like flowers and a graceful form make this a shrub difficult to surpass.*

Fremontodendron 'California Glory' Brilliant yellow blooms continue throughout the summer on this quick-growing wall shrub. ○, E, 6m/20ft

Cestrum elegans 'Smithii' Inclined to be tender so in need of wall protection. ○, E, 3m/10ft

Solanum jasminoides 'Album' An exceedingly lovely climber. This form, 'Album', is probably without equal. ○, semi-E, 6m/20ft

Passiflora caerulea The well-known passion flower is a vigorous grower. Small orange fruits follow the exquisite blooms. ○, 6m/20ft

Fremontodendron mexicanum Flowers appear a little more starry than those of 'California Glory'. ○, E, 6m/20ft

◆ *This is one of the longest blooming wall shrubs that can be grown – from late spring to mid-autumn.*

Passiflora 'Constance Elliott' This form is arguably lovelier with creamy white flowers. Like the above, needs watering in full growth but good drainage. ○, 6m/20ft

4. Climbers with Added Interest

Marvellous scents, autumnal fruits, eye-catching flowers and interesting leaves bring all-year appeal.

PLANTS *with* PERFUME

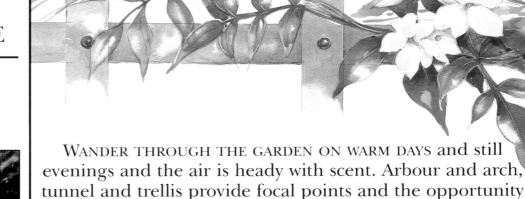

WANDER THROUGH THE GARDEN ON WARM DAYS and still evenings and the air is heady with scent. Arbour and arch, tunnel and trellis provide focal points and the opportunity for cascading canopies of fragrant climbers.

Akebia quinata An interesting, free-growing climber, exceedingly fragrant, but requiring the shelter of a wall. ○, 9m/30ft

Cytisus battandieri Smelling of pineapple, the Moroccan broom is an outstanding shrub to train against a wall. ○, semi-E, 4m/13ft

Wisteria floribunda **'Multijuga'** is noted for its long racemes which are beautiful when left to hang free. ○, 9m/30ft

Lathyrus odoratus **'Catherine'** Surely every garden should play host to the original sweet peas. ○, 2m/6ft

Clematis armandii A most welcome sight in the early spring, not least for the powerful scent. E, ○, 4.5m/15ft

Given sufficient space the common jasmine, *Jasminum officinale*, will delight with its clusters of trumpet flowers. In this setting the perfume is doubly intoxicating for the jasmine is combined with the enticingly fragrant *Rosa* **'Ena Harkness'**.

PLANTS *with* PERFUME

PROPAGATION

It is not difficult to increase stocks of the majority of honeysuckles. Plants may be either layered or multiplied by cuttings.

Layering involves bending a young shoot to come into contact with the earth. It is sometimes helpful to weight the stem with a stone. After a period of six months or so, roots will have formed and the layered stem may be separated from the parent plant.

Cuttings are best taken in summer and placed in a cold frame.

Lonicera × americana
Encourage this sweetly scented honeysuckle to climb with support wires. 7m/23ft

Lonicera periclymenum **'Belgica'** An early-flowering variety which is particularly fragrant on a warm, still night. 7m/23ft

Lonicera etrusca Long, branching flower panicles clothe an old brick wall in creamy yellow touched with red. Not hardy. ○, 4m/13ft

Lonicera japonica **'Halliana'** Fast growing with evergreen foliage and perfumed flowers in summer. E, 4m/13ft

SURROUND A SITTING-OUT AREA WITH FRAGRANT CLIMBERS trained up house walls, up posts or specially constructed pyramids. Honeysuckles with their heavenly scents are particular favourites.

PLANTS *with* PERFUME

***Lonicera periclymenum* 'Serotina'** Purplish-crimson flowers, the insides of which are cream, carry an enticing perfume. 7m/23ft

◆ *Most honeysuckles enjoy full sun or semi-shade and are unfussy about soil conditions.*

Lonicera periclymenum The common honeysuckle should not be overlooked, not least for its pronounced scent in the evening. 7m/23ft

Actinidia chinensis, the Chinese gooseberry, produces these handsome kiwi fruits in a warm area where both sexes are grown together. A companion planting of **Schisandra rubriflora** is in fruit with a berry not dissimilar to a large redcurrant.

A plant of *Actinidia chinensis* will grow to around 6m/20ft. *Schizandra rubriflora* at around 2.7m/9ft would make an elegant covering for an archway.

FRUITS, EDIBLE OR OTHERWISE, produced by some climbers add a further dimension to an attractive and interesting plant. Placed in full sunlight ornamental fruits will glow with vitality and life, a feature in themselves.

Vines make indispensable climbers, to be grown in both formal and informal situations, preferring sun but tolerating some shade. Fruits are seldom edible but are always ornamental. Many varieties possess handsome leaves and fabulous autumn tints.

Vitis vinifera 'Purpurea' Clusters of blue-black grapes form against leaves of purplish tints. 7m/23ft

Humulus lupulus 'Aureus' A splendid, vigorous foliage plant. 6m/20ft

◆ *Trusses of golden hops form in the autumn.*

SOMETHING UNUSUAL

THERE ARE PLANTS OF SUCH PROVEN WORTH that no garden should be without them. Others may demand a little extra care and attention, perhaps particular soil or shelter from cold winds, but if their requirements are met they will become a source of endless pleasure and delight.

Lathyrus rotundifolius
Attractive foliage and brick-red flowers are the mark of this perennial pea. 2m/6ft

Aristolochia durior An extraordinary flower accounting for its name as the Dutchman's pipe. 9m/30ft

◆ *An effective green column can be achieved by training* Aristolochia *around a pole.*

Lonicera tragophylla This honeysuckle is perhaps the most glamorous of all, but it has no scent. 6m/20ft

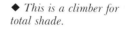
◆ *This is a climber for total shade.*

Jasminum* × *stephanense
Light pink flowers are displayed above leaves which often show some variegation. ◯, 7m/23ft

Trachelospermum jasminoides A woody climber with scented flowers in summer followed by long seed pods. E, 9m/30ft

Malvastrum lateritium is not so much a climber as a trailing perennial. Terracotta flowers have brick-red eyes. ◯, 1.2m/4ft

◆ *Show it off by allowing it to climb into the lower reaches of neighbouring shrubs.*

MANY GARDEN-WORTHY SHRUBS will respond well to being given a different treatment and trained to grow against a wall or fence. Some, indeed, will benefit and produce bigger flowers over a longer period.

Buddleja davidii will be perfectly happy tied into a wall or fence to produce a spectacular floral display. ○, 2.4m/8ft

Ceanothus 'Trewithen Blue' Best grown against a wall where the intense blue flowers will be displayed to effect. E, 2m/6ft

Pittosporum All forms of this attractive, evergreen shrub benefit from the protection of a wall or fence. E, 2.4m/8ft

Escallonia 'Iveyi' Compact shrub with large racemes of scented white flowers mid- to late summer. E, 3m/10ft

Leptospermum scoparium 'Alfred Coates' This New Zealand tea tree flowers late spring to summer. E, 3m/10ft

Lavatera maritima bicolor Tree mallows give both height and interest in the border. 1.5m/5ft

◆ *Take cuttings in case it dies in winter.*

SHRUBS *as* CLIMBERS

TIME AND TROUBLE TAKEN TO SECURE SHRUBS against hosts will result in better grown plants. Fixings should be checked annually and fastenings should not be allowed to cut into the stems.

Mahonia aquifolium is a deservedly popular evergreen, seen here carrying clusters of deep purple berries. E, 2m/6ft

Drimys lanceolata A splendid shrub to site against a wall. Creamy flowers are borne in early summer. E, 3m/10ft

Olearia cheesemanii Downy undersides to the leaves are a feature of this handsome, white-flowering shrub. 2.4m/8ft

Itea ilicifolia should be trained against a warm wall. E, 2.7m/9ft

◆ *These fragrant racemes appear mid- to late summer.*

***Philadelphus* 'Belle Etoile'** This form of the mock orange, trained here against a wall, is a mass of fragrant flowers in midsummer. ○, 2.4m/8ft

◆ *After flowering prune fairly severely to encourage new, long shoots.*

Hydrangea quercifolia The oak-loafed hydrangea has beautiful leaves and flowers midsummer to autumn. 2m/6ft

Azara serrata Not altogether hardy, this pretty shrub will repay time and care taken to grow it well. E, 2m/6ft

Chimonanthus praecox Winter sweet is, as its name suggests, wonderfully scented and lovely when cut for indoors. 2.4m/8ft

***Euonymus fortunei* 'Silver Queen'** has exceedingly attractive variegated foliage becoming creamier as the year progresses. E, 2.4m/8ft

SHRUBS *as* CLIMBERS

Mimulus glutinosus Given a sunny position and moisture retentive soil this mimulus should thrive in most gardens. 1.2m/4ft

***Magnolia grandiflora* 'Exmouth'** will in time make a splendid wall shrub. Large, scented flowers are an added bonus. ○, E, 9m/30ft

***Abelia* 'Edward Goucher'** Wall protection suits this sun-loving shrub. Dark pink flowers make for a late show. 2m/6ft

Cotoneaster horizontalis naturally grows in a fan-like shape and is covered in berries throughout the autumn. 2m/6ft

***Camellia* 'Waterlily'** Given acid soil camellias will perform well. ◑, E, 2m/6ft

◆ *Camellia flowers need protection from morning sun after frost.*

SHRUBS *as* CLIMBERS

INTERESTING RESULTS AND EFFECTS will be achieved in the garden when uncommon or unusual shrubs are treated in a less traditional manner. Providing stems and branches are not brittle, training subjects to grow against a wall is not a difficult task.

Abutilon megapotamicum Well worth growing for an abundance of conspicuous red and yellow flowers. E, 2.4m/8ft

◆ *To succeed this shrub requires the warmth of a wall in full sun.*

Abutilon vitifolium **'Album'** This white form has flowers not unlike those of a hollyhock. ◯, 2.4m/8ft

Hoheria lyallii A graceful shrub whose cool white flowers will enhance any border scheme. ◯, 4.5m/15ft

Phygelius capensis has unusually but effectively here been trained against a sunny wall. ◯, 2.4m/8ft

Robinia kelseyi is not always easy to train as the branches are inclined to break easily. ◯, 2.4m/8ft

Feijoa sellowiana Totally exotic in every way. The Pineapple guava sometimes produces edible fruits later in the year. ◯, E, 2.4m/8ft

Abeliophyllum distichum will reward in the late winter with delightfully fragrant starry flowers. ◯, 1.5m/5ft

Callistemon rigidus These 'bottle brushes' are an absolute delight and are carried above lemon-scented foliage. E, 3m/10ft

◆ *Callistemon must be grown in well drained, acid soil in a sunny position.*

5. TENDER CLIMBERS

Cold-sensitive climbers will transform a conservatory or glasshouse with a wealth of exciting flowers.

ALL *in a* YEAR

IN COLD AREAS, LIABLE TO FROSTS, a number of perennial climbers may be grown as annuals. In this way the range of subjects to be included in the garden scheme is greatly increased. With some protection, many of these climbers may prove to be hardier than was previously thought.

Tropaeolum tuberosum A striking climber which, as its name suggests, arises from an underground tuber. ○, 1.5m/5ft

◆ *Lift tubers in autumn, cover with silver sand and store in a cool place.*

Rhodochiton atrosanguineus A most intriguing and utterly striking climber from Mexico with strange red and purple flowers. ○, 3m/10ft

◆ *Following the flowers, interest is maintained with balloon-like seed capsules.*

Jasminum polyanthum is deliciously scented and will thrive in a cool conservatory. Keep away from direct heat. E, 2.7m/9ft+

Eccremocarpus scaber
Popularly known as the
Chilean glory vine, it is
noted for its orange and
yellow flowers. ○, 4m/13ft

***Eccremocarpus scaber
coccineus*** A red form with
typical tubular flowers.
Easily raised from seed. ○,
4m/13ft

Plumbago capensis is
happiest when left to
scramble amongst other
plantings. Hard prune in
spring. ○, 4m/13ft

***Solanum crispum* 'Glasnevin'** Rich purple
potato-like flowers single out this
particular form. Frost-hardy to –5°C/23°F.
○, E or semi-E, 6m/20ft

◆ *Although technically a shrub,
solanum is nearly always wall-trained.*

Displays such as this are not difficult if a little trouble is taken. The outdoor garden is extended when favoured climbers like these are grown. Here the sumptuous flowers of the passion flower **Passiflora antioquiensis** tone with the pure blue flowers, rare in the garden, of **Tweedia caerulea** (also known as *Oxypetalum*). Nearby **Lapageria rosea** (the Chilean bellflower) displays evergreen heart-shaped leaves to show off beautiful waxy, crimson-pink, bell-shaped flowers. The tweedia will reach up to 1.2m/4ft whilst the passion flower and Chilean bellflower can go above 5m/16ft.

Mutisia ilicifolia Mauve-pink daisy flowers will bloom from spring onwards. E, 3m/10ft

◆ *Keep dry in winter.*

CONSERVATORIES ARE THE TRADITIONAL HOME of many of the half-hardy species which are so exciting and such a delight to cultivate. A number simply require a frost-free environment; others should be given heat to maintain a minimum temperature.